TRUE HERITAGE
RECOVERING FROM SPIRITUAL IDENTITY THEFT

D.L. FULLER

Palmetto Publishing Group
Charleston, SC

True Heritage
Copyright © 2019 by D.L. Fuller

First Edition

Printed in the United States

Paperback: 9781641114578
Hardcover: 9781641114097
eBook: 9781641114561

Dedicated to Shaina, Jah'Son, Amari, and Andrew.
Remember to always live in spirit and truth,
rooted in your identity as children of YAHWEH.

TABLE OF CONTENTS

INTRODUCTION

I woke up this morning thinking about the bastardizing of men. Bastardize means "to change by integrating opposing elements." That is exactly what man allowed the serpent to do in the Garden of Eden. Adam, the first man, was made after the image of love, for God is Love. Adam allowed the serpent, a.k.a. the devil, to sow a seed of doubt into his heart. Doubt leads to fear, and there is no fear in love. This doubt caused Adam and his descendants to be bastardized. When you hear the phrase "born in sin," this is a direct reference to the skew created when mankind was bastardized in the Garden. Man became a "GMO," a genetically modified organism, to borrow a term used to describe much of the food we are sold today. This marked the fall of man, since it caused a distortion in the image man was formed to reflect.

This change in man's heart caused him to become alienated from his Heavenly Father. The seed of doubt grew and replaced the faith needed to walk with God. A doubting heart is a closed heart, and a closed heart cannot receive. The doubt interfered with man's ability to receive seeds of love in his heart. This stopped the harvesting of the fruits love: righteousness, peace, and joy. The godly heritage that was supposed to permeate mankind had been corrupted.

Bastardized man thinks mostly of himself, without consideration for those who follow, his descendants. So, he does not embrace the potency or essence of a heritage. Heritage is what preserves an order, or way of living. Heritage makes a people strong, viable, and united. Without a sense of heritage, every man lives predominantly for himself. Bastards don't care about protecting a lineage in order to preserve a sustainable heritage. This is what God informs us of in 2 Timothy 3:1–5 (KJV):

> This know also, that in the last days perilous times shall come. For men shall be lovers of their own selves, covetous, boasters, proud, blasphemers, disobedient to parents, unthankful, unholy, without natural affection, truce breakers, false accusers, incontinent, fierce, despisers of those that are good, traitors, heady, high minded, lovers of pleasures more than lovers of God; Having a form of godliness, but denying the power thereof: from such turn away.

Any people without a heritage will self destruct. Heritage provides the explanation for why is it so important to stay united and to persevere. The character traits described in 2 Timothy 3:1–5 are characteristic of most men today. We live in a generation of bastards; the generation of the fatherless.

This sense of heritage is so important to God that it is the main reason He choose Abraham. In Genesis, chapter 18, God says He chose Abraham because He knew Abraham would be faithful to keep His heritage of righteousness, justice, and judgment alive for generations to come. God knew Abraham would be faithful to watch over His name by teaching his children and descendants the ways of the Lord. Where there is no sense of heritage, the vision is lost, the purpose is lost, and the generations are lost. The way of the Lord is the salt that preserves the generations. The heritage of the Lord is what sustains mankind. Truth is . . . mankind wasn't intended to be mankind at all. Mankind was created to be *godkind*. The powers of darkness have been on a relentless offensive to remove the traces of godliness from man in order to destroy the generations of man. Thanks and glory be unto God who has prevailed through the life of Yeshua the Savior, to establish a way for man to redeemed and restored to his true heritage, and to walk again in the image of God.

Chapter 1

THE FEAR OF THE LORD

Proverbs 1:7 (KJV) reads, "The fear of the Lord is the beginning of knowledge: but fools despise wisdom and instruction."

Psalm 110:10 (KJV) reads, "The fear of the LORD is the beginning of wisdom: a good understanding have all they that do his commandments: his praise endureth for ever."

Proverbs 2:4–6 (KJV) reads, "If thou seekest her as silver, and searchest for her as for hid treasures; Then shalt thou understand the fear of the Lord, and find the knowledge of God. For the Lord giveth wisdom: out of his mouth cometh knowledge and understanding."

The fear of the Lord is the frame that holds the picture of God. You cannot begin to understand the first things of God until you have a frame of reference from which to approach His Gloriousness. Without the framing of the fear of the Lord, you will lack the proper perspective to prioritize even the most miniscule things of God. It is easy for someone not understanding the fear of the Lord to forsake some detail of God as trivial, not realizing it will tip the scale and unbalance their life.

Verse 25 in chapter 1 of 1 Corinthians (KJV) reads, "The foolishness of God is wiser than men; and the weakness of God is stronger than men."

The fear of the Lord teaches you your place in respect to the one by which all things are sustained. The whole of creation is the product of His brilliance, and all things have purpose according to

1

His design. This is why it is of vital importance to understand the correct order of things, to avoid vanity, perversion, and destruction.

The Lord Yeshua explains in John 14:6 (KJV), "I am the way, the truth, and the life."

God is reality. Anything outside of God is mere deception, and not real at all. To seek God is to seek life. When you are seeking God, you are seeking all things, because He is the beginning and conclusion of all things that are real. When you have the right perspective from the fear of the Lord, you understand that the knowledge and wisdom of God is the key to enjoying creation to the fullest. Those unlearned in the fear of the Lord seek creation more than the creator and squander the intended blessings of creation. God made creation so good that even its misuse brings a small level of enjoyment. I say "a small level" because the shallow enjoyment experienced through unenlightened experimentation is nothing compared to the deep fulfillment experienced by those instructed in the fear of the Lord, who have humbled themselves to live according to the Creator's design. When true purpose is fulfilled, the experience is optimized. The fulfillment of the soul is made possible by the enlightenment of the spirit. In order to save the world, Yeshua came to restore that light.

The book of John begins with a teaching on the fear of the Lord. It reads, "In the beginning was the Word, and the Word was with God, and the Word was God. He was in the beginning with God. All things were made through Him, and without Him nothing was made that was made. In Him was life, and the life was the light of men" (John 1:1–4 KJV).

The fear of the Lord is the first illumination. Once you begin to understand creation after the fear of the Lord, then instruction can begin. There is no randomness about creation. Everything fits together according to a specific design and function. There is definite order and relationship in creation. Creation tells us many things about the Creator, because creation is an expression of the Creator. Creation is even reflective of the Creator. One could no more dismiss the relationship between a piece of art and the mind of an artist, than creation from the mind of the Creator. Unfortunately, people who don't understand the fear of the Lord make this mistake every day. Though creation is specific, ordered, and intentional, many unenlightened people speak of the Almighty God as if He is actually many different things to many different people instead of someone specific, with an order, and distinct. The problem here is that people define God as they see fit, instead of humbling themselves to accept God's definition of himself. The hidden motive of the rebellious and prideful is to allow room for them to define themselves, instead of humbling themselves to conform to God's definition of them. This is at the root of why people use anamorphic names like "the man upstairs" and "my higher power" to refer to their deity. I say "their deity," because actually they aren't referring to the Almighty at all. They are actually referring to the deity in their mind, which they have concocted, that fits their way of living. People may not actively seek out forgers of metal and carvers of wood to custom design their deities any longer, but people very much still form images in their mind of a God they are comfortable with, and make that image their deity. You can easily have in the same room a Mormon, a Klu Klux Klan member, a homosexual, a Jehovah Witnesses, a Seventh-day Adventist, a Catholic priest, and a transvestite who all confess that they know God and serve Him. This conundrum is due to an overall lack in understanding the fear of the Lord. Conforming to the universal standards and principles of the Creator is more important and vital than conforming to individual appetites and ambitions. The fear of the Lord teaches that instead of defaming the character, nature, and image of God, to comply with the preferences of any one person or group, we must humbly conform to the one true and living God. This is what Yeshua spoke of when He said, "If any man will come after me, let him deny himself, and take up his cross, and follow me." (Matthew 16:24 KJV). It is also what Yeshua is referring to when He says, "For whosoever will save his life shall lose it: and whosoever will lose his life for my sake shall find it." (Matthew 16:25 KJV). fear of the Lord. The fear of the Lord teaches that God is life, and we should seek our existence in Him, for outside of God there is only death. Anything that opposes God, inherently opposes life, and should be considered evil. Proverbs 8:13 (KJV) says, "The fear of the Lord is to hate evil: pride, and arrogancy, and the evil way, and the froward mouth, do I hate."

Pride and arrogance should be hated, because those characteristics support and strengthen self-reliance, instead of reliance on God.

Many people object to the view that we should fear a loving God. Those who feel this way often say the Bible is only referring to a reverential fear, and not a sense of terror. Rejecting the concept that we should actually fear God—based on the idea the word "fear" in the phrase "the fear of the Lord" was mistranslated—is evil in root; evil, because it refuses to surrender its humanistic ideas of God. God Himself says we should dread opposing Him, and scripture strongly supports that there is virtue in fearing God. It is very true that God is a loving God, but it is also true that God will recompense evil. God hates evil, and regularly destroys it. The Almighty God is terrible and fearful. He is not one to be played with or provoked. The Apostle Paul says in Hebrews 10:31 (KJV), "It is a fearful thing to fall into the hands of the living God."

In Hebrews, chapter 10, Paul is trying to make sure that we do not forsake the fear of the Lord in this dispensation of amazing grace, after the sacrifice of Christ. Paul is warning us not to take God for granted, as if God is going to remit the sins we continue to commit willingly, after we know better.

Yeshua taught in Matthew 10:28 (KJV), "Fear not them which kill the body, but are not able to kill the soul: but rather fear him which is able to destroy both soul and body in hell."

This is New Testament teaching on the Fear of the Lord by God Himself. Proverbs 16:6 (KJV) says, "By mercy and truth iniquity is purged: and by the fear of the LORD men depart from evil."

Through the mercies of God, truth is revealed. There is a lot of preparing of the heart that takes place by the hand of God before the truth is sown, much like a farmer prepares the earth for a crop he wants to harvest. The fear of the Lord restrains men from evil, which keeps them alive while the truth takes root, and the iniquity is purged. It is the fear of the Lord that makes man teachable. It is my hope that the teachings of this book will build upon your foundation of the fear of the Lord, toward a deeper and more fulfilling relationship with God.

Chapter 2

RECOVERING THE IMAGE

What Drives You?

There are universal laws and principles at work in the world around us. The physical world we see is really a shadow of the spiritual. When we begin to understand the spiritual laws at work in the universe, we see that natural laws are merely consequential. Everything is actually spiritual in root. To have a true understanding of who you are, you need to understand the spiritual influences around you. A look at things in the light of the spirit will tell us more about who it is we believe we are, and why.

Many people base who they are on the behavior that comes natural to them. A better understanding of what drives the natural could reveal a lot about our behaviors. The person you think you are could very easily be based on spiritual puppetry, where you are the puppet. Another way of looking at this is psychological, or mental manipulation, based on ideas and thought patterns ingrained through exterior suggestion. The majority of the people in the world have been subjected to this type of manipulation. What most people call "freedom" is, in effect, slavery, because they are being controlled by influences they are not aware of. When Yeshua read the prophecy of Isaiah, as recorded in the book of Luke, chapter 4:18 (KJV), He stated, "He was anointed...to preach deliverance to the captives." People are captive, and don't realize it.

The Pharaoh of the Old Testament is a physical representation of the devil. The bondage and oppression he inflicted on the children of Israel is a glimpse into the spiritual workings of the devil. Moses, the deliverer, is a physical representation of Yeshua. Moses represents the power of God sent to liberate His people, so that they could fulfill their destiny as His people. Many of the perceptions and ideas that shape the behavior of the masses are rooted in lies spun by the devil. Horoscopes are a great example. God put man in the earth, and gave him dominion over it. Horoscopes suggest that physicality has dominion over us. Jesus said in John 8:32 (KJV), "Ye shall know the truth and the truth shall make you free."

The knowledge of the truth has the potential to change us by delivering us from false perceptions and ideas that influence behavior.

The False Self

The self-image carried by most people is derived from the internalization of experiences incurred from the world. People adapt behaviors that are conducive to outcomes they feel they desire or need. Those that control the things we feel we need or desire, have the greatest influence in shaping who we become. Good parents will use that influence to shape their children into virtuous people. Bad parents spoil the character of a child by not affirming the association of good behavior with rewards and privileges. Similarly, this world system ingrains ideas about "the good life" and "happiness" on the population, and then shape their behavior as they strive to achieve them. When you have millions of people indoctrinated into an ideology, there is plenty of consensus to reinforce the idea. These worldly ideas eventually become beliefs. People will conform to be accepted into the majority. When there is inner conflict with external popular behavior, people feel the need to adapt, to avoid jeopardizing what they have come to believe will bring happiness.

They bury the feelings of dissonance, and then adopt a morality that doesn't make them feel bad about their actions. They try to muffle that inner guide. Our conscience is very persistent, though, and these types of compromises disrupt inner peace.

As the circumstances of life expose our inner conflicts and brokenness, we can either come to terms with the need to change, or find a way to numb the noise of the disharmony inside. People use the anesthesia of drugs, food, sex, movies, gaming, hurting themselves, violence, or the self-deception of "I don't care." We can all probably look back on some of our past deeds and feel nauseated as we think to ourselves, *How could I have done that?* We may look at our current situation and think, *How did I get to this place?*

When people habitually ignore the inner voice of their conscience, they become something unnatural. They become something foreign to who they were created to be. The effective conditioning of a carnal world has oriented the masses toward their fleshy desires. This is mainly for capitalization, predictability, and control. The Word of God tells us to be in the world, but not of the world. We are to be in this carnal world; however, we are to maintain our spiritual disposition. When we are carnal, it is not a representation of our true selves. Your true self is spiritual.

God's plan, as creator of all living, was to father an existence of children that had His holy nature, and would therefore automatically operate in divine order, generating life. A spiritual law that is in effect in our universe is that the seed will bear fruit after its kind. When we were originally created, God brought us out of Himself. We see in the book of Genesis when God created beast, He called to the earth, and when He created fish, He called to the sea, but when He created man, He called to himself. He is the seed, and we are the fruit. The problem occurred when we were genetically modified in the Garden of Eden by sin. Every man between Adam and Jesus was born with the birth defect of sin.

The Burden of the Father

I would like to focus on the father in the family as being the seed bearer. It is the father's responsibility to ensure that his likeness or kind is preserved for all time. It is the father's responsibility to secure a lasting legacy, and to preserve a heritage for generations to follow. The main way a father does this is by ensuring that his fruit understands who they are based on their heritage. As a young boy begins to frame his perception of manhood, he will undoubtedly try to identify with his father. The son will open his heart to his father to receive instruction. If the boy's father has accepted the seed of God, through the salvation of Christ, then he will have divine seed to sow into the heart of his son. As a man is fathered by God, God sows into him all he needs to be a father. The man is then able to reciprocate this down into his own son. A father does not have to be flawless in order to share the seed of God as good father. A father only needs to be transparent about his fierce dedication to reflect God's love in raising the child. The rest God will take care of.

To sow the seed properly, the father must have intimate access to the heart of his children. This is no easy task. A relationship of trust must exist before the child will open the heart to truly receive. The child must be assured of the father's love. Once the seed has been sown, it must be left undisturbed until it has had time to root. Once it is set, it will eventually bear fruit. However, if it is uprooted through doubt and unbelief, it will not bear fruit. This is what happened to Adam. Satan was able to uproot the seed of God from Adam's heart. Satan was able to dissuade Adam of God's perfect unchanging love for him. This new seed of doubt took root and blocked God's accessibility to Adam's heart. This is why Proverbs 4:23 (KJV) says, "Keep your heart with all diligence, for out of it are the issues of life."

Consequently, every man between Adam and Jesus has received a corrupted seed into his heart. When the true seed of God was lost, so was the image of God in mankind. True manhood resembles

9

godliness. How was God to get sons back into His own image? Thanks be to the Father who sent a new son into the earth bearing His perfect image, Yeshua the Christ. Yeshua, the only begotten son of the Father, not born of man but born of God. This is why the Bible refers to Yeshua as the second Adam.

> And so it is written, the first man Adam was made a living soul; the last Adam was made a quickening spirit. Howbeit that was not first which is spiritual, but that which is natural; and afterward that which is spiritual. The first man is of the earth, earthy; the second man is the Lord from heaven. As is the earthy, such are they also that are earthy: and as is the heavenly, such are they also that are heavenly. And as we have borne the image of the earthy, we shall also bear the image of the heavenly. (1 Corinthians 15:45–49 KJV)

Jesus is called the "express image" of God in Hebrews 1:1–3 (KJV): "God, who at various times and in various ways spoke in time past to the fathers by the prophets, has in these last days spoken to us by His Son, whom He has appointed heir of all things, through whom also He made the worlds; who being the brightness of His glory and the express image of His person."

The love of God is revealed to the world abroad through the person of Yeshua the Christ. When a man receives the message of Yeshua the Savior, his faith in the Love of God is restored. This faith, which works through the understanding that God truly loves us, allows a man to surrender his heart to the Father again. God takes away a man's stony and perverted heart, and then gives him a new hallowed heart. The promise of God through the Savior is the gift of a new heart. With this new heart, the perfect seed of God can be sown to restore the legacy and heritage of the God the Father. Now, through Yeshua, every man has access to the Father to get a new heart whereby the image of God can be restored. The book of John, chapter 1 (KJV) states, "To as many as received him gave he power to become the sons of God."

Once the new heart is received, and the seed is planted, it is up to the man to guard his heart. We must guard our hearts, and not allow the devil's lies or perversions to uproot it. Once the seed of God is allowed to take root in our hearts, it is incorruptible. Nothing can stop us from bearing good fruit! That is a bold statement, one you don't hear very often. If you will pause and take a moment to think about just who God is and what he is capable of, you will realize that it sounds just like the promise of an Almighty God. It sounds like a Heavenly Father with unlimited power. God has implemented a plan that is perfect. Maybe not perfect according to the understanding of some, but perfect according to the understanding of the perfect.

Chapter 3

THE LOVE OF THE FATHER

The Father Loves to Adopt

E veryone should experience the love of a godly father. If you have not, no worries, it is not too late if you are reading this. If your earthly father is not present for any reason, then the Lord will take care of you. Psalm 27:10–14 (KJV) says:

> When my father and my mother forsake me, then the LORD will take me up. Teach me thy way, O LORD, and lead me in a plain path, because of mine enemies. Deliver me not over unto the will of mine enemies: for false witnesses are risen up against me, and such as breathe out cruelty. I had fainted, unless I had believed to see the goodness of the LORD in the land of the living. Wait on the LORD: be of good courage, and he shall strengthen thine heart: wait, I say, on the LORD.

Parents, the mother and the father combined, are an archetype of God in relationship to their children. There are characteristics embodied in both the mother as a woman and the father as a man that reflects specific properties of the God-head. The God-head is God the Father, God the Holy Spirit, and God the Son. The care and protection given by parents to their children was intended by God to reflect His own care and concern for the wellbeing of His children, man. In those families where the parents neglect the children, it is due to the absence of God's seed in the hearts of the parents. What is important for you to know is that if you have had abusive or negligent parents, it is not your fault, because the abuse stems from experiences beyond your control. The command of God is that we love people based on how we would want to be loved; however, people often love others based on how they have been loved. The trail of broken relationships between parents and children can be traced back to its origin in the Garden of Eden to Adam and his relationship with God. God is Love, so parents can only love their own children to the degree they are able to receive God's love. Only God can create, so people cannot give what they have not received. Psalm 27:10–14 is a great scriptural illustration of what I have been writing about. The Lord will step in and take care of the child that cries out for Him. The Lord will strengthen the child's heart with the proper nurture of love and ensure that His seed is sown in their heart.

As stated in Psalm 27, the enemy has contrived a plan to bring about his own will concerning the life of the child which entails cruel and violent intentions. All through the Old Testament there are instances where Satan, the enemy, has brought false witness with the intention of getting between God and His children. Satan's main mechanism for bringing this to pass is by deceiving the people of God into believing and accepting an outcome different from what God promises. Satan's ultimate objective is always to kill, steal, and destroy everything that resembles God. The Lord wants to be a refuge for us against such plans in the same way our earthly parents should want to protect us from harm. When our earthly parents fail, the Lord is able to save us from the evil circumstances, and heal the brokenness in our hearts.

The Father Watches

One of God's loving gifts to us is freedom. Unfortunately, under the influence of Satan, this freedom is abused by people, often resulting in horrible crimes, but in the book of Isaiah 59:18 (KJV), it is written, "According to their deeds, accordingly He will repay, Fury to His adversaries, Recompense to His enemies."

Again, the Lord says in Isaiah 35:4 (KJV), "Say to them that are of a fearful heart, be strong, fear not: behold, your God will come with vengeance, even God with a recompense; he will come and save you."

In the New Testament, Yeshua says in Luke 17:2 (KJV), "It would be better for him if a millstone was hung around his neck, and he were thrown into the sea, than that he should offend one of these little ones."

Chronological age is not a factor in determining who is a little one, for God sees us all as children. What I am trying to illustrate here is how the heart of God is toward his children. I am also trying to show how it has always been the plan of the enemy to get between the Father and his children by perverting the message of God's love and intentions. That is why salvation is expressed in such an extravagant display of love: "For God so loved the world that he gave his only begotten son" (John 3:16 KJV).

After the revelation of the sacrifice of Yeshua on the Cross, no more questions should remain regarding God's love for mankind.

Christ and the Father's Love

Few earthly fathers understand their roll in preparing the hearts of their children to ultimately accept the love of the Heavenly Father. Our acceptance of God's love is ultimately the key to the restoration of divine order amongst mankind. Many men, as Psalm 27 suggests, have forsaken their seed and left them vulnerable to the will of the enemy.

In chapter 4 of the book of Malachi, verses 5–6 read, "Behold, I will send you Elijah the prophet before the coming of the great and dreadful day of the Lord: And he shall turn the heart of the fathers to the children, and the heart of the children to their fathers, lest I come and smite the earth with a curse."

This message is vital to the world, and it will be spread throughout the earth. There is so much that the Father has provided for His children to ensure that they prosper and are well, but many of us lack the faith to receive the provision due to believing the false witness of the wicked one. Many people feel outside of God's favor and love, therefore the things freely given to them of God seem unattainable. God declares He is not like negligent earthly parents. He wants to be seen in the true light of who He is. Unfortunately, the love that was meant to light the way has been extinguished in many. Yeshua came to restore that light.

The gospel of Christ illuminates God's love in a way that renews faith toward God and restores hope in God's promises. It is a daunting task to believe that the being who created the massive universe, in all of its wonder, has genuine love and concern for man individually, as well as collectively. What makes this so unbelievable is the rejection we receive from our fellow man. On earth, we see that we are physically alike, and see that we have the same needs, yet we hate and dehumanize one another. Some of these people who reject us and hurt us are family members we feel a definite connection to. So, carrying what you learned from those experiences, you try to process how the Supreme Being could love you, whom you have never seen, whom you strain to relate to, and it seems impossible. It is the wounds from the evil around us that stifle our ability to obtain unto the love of God. The amazing grace shown through the cross of Yeshua the Christ brings the Father's love within reach. The passion of Christ begins to stir us to the realization of God's divine love. It is also the divine love demonstrated by those born again through

Christ that bares further witness to the prevailing love of God the Father.

Parents cannot control the actions of others, but they can take responsibility for their own witness of God's parental love. Since parents are the archetype of God to the children, the hurt or rejection inflicted by them is substantially more detrimental to the development of a child's sense that God loves them. A vast amount of faith is not necessary to trust God and to believe in Him. It is the mountainous hurt and rejection that often fills the wounded human heart that makes it difficult to receive the love that streams from God. Faith works by the knowledge of God's love for us. The comprehension of God's love sustains the hope necessary to hold on and be patient until the unseen is obtained. The love administered through the cross of Christ regenerates the wounded heart enabling it to receive the love which pours from God. Once we are assured of God's love, we then have a firm foundation for standing on His promises. The rest is just waiting on God's timing. This is why Yeshua says if we have faith as a grain of mustard seed we can move mountains. The hard part is getting rid of the doubt created by the wounded heart. If no one had ever failed you, you would have a greater propensity to hope than someone who had been disappointed several times. I am not trying to say that believers are never disappointed. What I am saying is that there are some things promised by God that believers should never despair of, because God never fails, and He keeps all of His promises. Our task is to let all the old things pass away that we may have a greater ability to obtain unto the new.

We must forgive our parents of any debts we feel they owe us. Our parents are only older children dealing with the wounds afflicted upon their hearts. At some point we all have to take ownership over the gardens of our hearts, and decide what plants we will allow to grow, and what things we will root out. Most importantly, we have to decide what seed we will allow to enter our hearts because that determines what type of garden will grow. The type of garden that grows in our heart determines the fruit we will have in our life.

So, God's intent is to fill our hearts with His Word which will yield love and light, but first our hearts must be open to receive from God, which means we have to trust Him.

Chapter 4

BROKEN COMMUNICATION

The Message of the Cross

Genesis 8:22 (KJV) says, "While the earth remaineth, seedtime and harvest, and cold and heat, and summer and winter, and day and night shall not cease."

Seed time and harvest is an order that YAHWEH says will never cease, as long as the Earth remains. YAHWEH has sown a son into the earth that He might reap a harvest of sons. The gospel of John, chapter 1, verse 12 (KJV) reads, "But as many as received Him, to them He gave the right to become children of God, to those who believe in His name: who were born, not of blood, nor of the will of the flesh, nor of the will of man, but of God."

Yeshua came to restore the family of God. Man must grasp the strong yearning of God the Father for his children. It is a consistent theme throughout the Bible. That is what Yeshua is referring to in Matthew 23:37–39 (NKJV) when He says, "O Jerusalem, Jerusalem, the one who kills the prophets and stones those who are sent to her! How often I wanted to gather your children together, as a hen gathers her chicks under her wings, but you were not willing! See! Your house is left to you desolate; for I say to you, you shall see Me no more till you say, 'Blessed is He who comes in the name of the Lord!'"

YAHWEH says how often He would have gathered His people under His wings to protect them and hold them close however they refused Him. In Jeremiah 31:3 (NKJV), the prophet says that the Lord appeared unto him saying, "Yes, I have loved you with an everlasting love; therefore with loving kindness I have drawn you."

YAHWEH, throughout the Old Testament, referred to the children of Israel as His people.

Verse 11, chapter 10 in 1 Corinthians states, "Now all these things happened unto them for examples: and they are written for our admonition, upon whom the ends of the world are come" (KJV).

The interactions between YAHWEH and the children of Israel were examples to us that we should take heed too. YAHWEH loves us, and wants us to identify with Him as children to their father. His arms are outstretched toward us. Whenever I hear "outstretched arms" in reference to the standing invitation of our Father, my heart recalls renderings of Christ on the cross. Truly this was an invitation to all men to come unto Him, to pass through His death to life. In the sufferings of Christ, the Father's love found its greatest expression. In John 15:13 (KJV), Yeshua says, "Greater love hath no man than this, that a man lay down his life for his friends."

The sufferings of Christ were for you and me.

Isaiah 53:4–6 (KJV) reads, "Surely He has borne our griefs and carried our sorrows; He was wounded for our transgressions, He was bruised for our iniquities; The chastisement for our peace was upon Him, by His stripes we are healed."

Way before the movie *The Passion of the Christ,* the scriptures revealed to me the brutality of Christ's sufferings. In the midst of an in-depth study of Isaiah 53:4–6, I found myself weeping in sorrow as the reality of what Christ endured for me was unveiled by the Spirit of Truth. As part of my study, I searched the Hebrew Concordance for the original words from which the words "wounded," "bruised," and "stripes" were translated, and I got meanings like "to crush, crumble, or beat to pieces"; "to be made sick or weak from strain, afflicted." A desire to be reconnected with His children and to have them restored to righteousness, peace, and joy is what made the brutality of the cross worthwhile. God has been trying to communicate this love to us for all of history but communication has been broken.

Communication, Minus the Hearing

For communication to work successfully there must be a transmission and a receipt. God has been faithful with his transmissions; the problem has been on the receiving end.

Proper communication consists of a transmission and then an acknowledgement of the transmission to confirm receipt. Due to the high levels of pride and selfishness that exist today in the hearts of men, there are many more looking to be heard than are willing to listen. Communication is ineffective without good listening. Though we live in the age of information there is comparatively little understanding. This is due to the overall poor communication skills of the populous. Understanding is reached through good communication.

When a social environment is laden with strife and contention, the culprit is most often broken communication; more specifically it is poor listening on the part of one or both parties. Pride is the number one cause of poor listening. Pride tells a person what he is saying and thinking is so much more important and relevant than what someone else is expressing. Pride causes you to listen only in part to someone else, or to not listen at all. The half listening occurs when you are thinking about what you are going to say next while someone else is speaking to you, either because you assume you already know the complete thought they are trying to relay, or because you are not interested. Instead of listening to them, you are just waiting on them to finish so you can say what you are pressed to say.

There are times when people won't even let you finish speaking before they start to respond. When a person does not listen at all, it is due to an unwillingness to even entertain a different view or idea other than the one they already hold. This type of closed-mindedness often occurs when the idea being offered threatens or contends with a deep belief that is foundational to a particular mind-set, behavior, or a person's identity. In other words, the closed person is thinking, *You are not going to change me, or the way I think, because nothing is wrong with me.*

The new idea threatens to bring about an unwanted change. The unwanted change could be a new view of oneself that makes them less appealing. The unwanted change could be the end of an enjoyed behavior. A change in thinking could mean the admittance that they have been wrong. A mature person would be willing to make the exchange regardless of what it required, if it brought them closer to the truth. The immature person, due to incorrect values, would have a tendency to love the temporal comfort and pleasure more than truth. This brings us to the heart of problem with broken communication between God and man.

Ignoring the Truth

The word of YAHWEH is truth. Truth, when it is expressed, immediately confronts all falsehoods and demands acknowledgement. Truth is the law and fabric of reality. Everything not in line with truth is out of order and false. Now, from the statements above, it easy to see that truth can create conflict. Conflicts are often settled by people in authority. There would be little conflict with truth if it was always heard from the mouth of God to the hearers. No one in their right mind would resist or argue with God. The issue comes because God chooses men to share His truth, and while sane people wouldn't challenge God, they challenge their fellow man without hesitating. People contend with other people all the time. People often know truth when they hear it, but will contend with it in a perverse effort to hold onto to something they love more. Conflicting truth is often disqualified on the basis that no one can prove that it actually came from God, therefore it lacks proper authority.

This is why YAHWEH often sends His messengers of truth with signs and wonder. Especially in the face of strong resistance to truth. The signs and wonders affirm that the messenger represents the authority of YAHWEH. Today, there is not a lot of resistance to hearing the truth, there is just a hideous an overwhelming tolerance for ignoring the truth. This tendency of ignoring truth comes from a love of comfort and pleasure. The rationalizations used to justify the ignoring of truth create a dependency on perverted reasoning, which leads to the reprobate mind. The reprobate mind has no capacity for the Word of YAHWEH. So, we see that a love of pleasure and comfort can lead to broken communication with God.

Source of the Interference

A love of pleasure and comfort can lead to resisting the change required in acknowledging truth. This is why it is good to practice fasting. Fasting helps to keep a check on our carnal appetites. Fasting can be a great aid for calibrating our hearing, and for strengthening our resolve to live in truth. The scripture says all that is in the world is the lust of the flesh, the lust of the eye, and the pride of life. Another way to say this would be, "All that is in the world is lust, empowered by a sense of entitlement, which leads to deafening bondage. Discipline alone, however, is not enough to restore our hearing. Matthew 6:22 (KJV) says, "The light of the body is the eye: if therefore thine eye be single, thy whole body shall be full of light."

In the book of John, we learn that the Truth became flesh, and dwelt among men. We learn that Truth incarnate proclaimed that He was the Light of the world. This was none other than Yeshua the Christ. To restore communication with YAHWEH, a person has to be convinced that Yeshua was God manifested in the earth, and then

seek Him first above all else. Doing this ascribes supreme authority to the Gospel of Christ. This removes the contention of other
things from our focus on the Truth of God. Accepting Christ as the
Salvation of God is more than a mere confession with our lips. The
real confession is what we express through the actions of our life.
A confession based on sincere belief, evidenced through a changed
life that is progressing towards godliness. Until a person reaches the
reality of Yeshua as the Salvation of God, that person will always
waver forwards and backwards, never obtaining the maturity that
comes from acknowledging the truth, as stated in 2 Timothy 3:1–8
(NKJV):

> But know this, that in the last days perilous times will
> come: For men will be lovers of themselves, lovers of
> money, boasters, proud, blasphemers, disobedient to
> parents, unthankful, unholy, unloving, unforgiving,
> slanderers, without self-control, brutal, despisers of
> good, traitors, headstrong, haughty, lovers of plea-
> sure rather than lovers of God, having a form of god-
> liness but denying its power. And from such people
> turn away! For of this sort are those who creep into
> households and make captives of gullible women load-
> ed down with sins, led away by various lusts, always
> learning and never able to come to the knowledge of
> the truth. Now as Jannes and Jambres resisted Moses,
> so do these also resist the truth: men of corrupt minds,
> disapproved concerning the faith.

Broken communication with God means no capacity to love. No
capacity to love means lacking the capacity to have genuine concern
for others. A person in this state becomes overrun with selfish vices.
Communication cannot be restored until the power of selfishness is
broken. Faith comes by hearing, hearing comes by the Word of God,
and the Word of God comes by a love of truth. A love of truth comes

after a man takes up his cross to follow Yeshua. Communication is restored by embracing God in the face of Yeshua the Christ. Yeshua is the seed of Love that has to be sown in every man's heart to restore communication with God.

Chapter 5

WHEN LOVE CALLS, LET TRUST ANSWER

There Are Prerequisites

Hebrews 11:6 (KJV) states, "But without faith it is impossible to please him; for he that comes to God must believe that he is, and that he is a rewarder of them that diligently seeks him."

In John, chapter 4, verses 23–24 (KJV) say, "But the hour cometh, and now is, when the true worshippers shall worship the Father in spirit and in truth: for the Father seeketh such to worship him. God is a Spirit: and they that worship him must worship him in spirit and in truth."

We cannot just come to God in any way. The scripture teaches us that God resists the proud. If the journey to God begins with a passageway that causes you to bow down, and you refuse to bend your knees or lower your head, how can you progress? You cannot. How can one begin to seek God while they feel they are everything and complete within themselves? It is very common to even hear people say that they are trying to find themselves. The pursuit of God cannot begin until we are aware that we are just a part of something bigger than ourselves, and then we must believe that that something bigger is definite and identifiable. Seeking God begins with the hope of finding Him. To come to God, you must have a sincere hope of finding Him, and an expectation that He will satisfy your yearning. We need to also realize that the invitation to come as you are is not an invitation to *stay* as you are. The necessity to change is not a rejection of you, but a necessary consequence of revealing the real you. To seek God is to seek truth, so with seeking God there needs to be a readiness to turn from the false. The false has to be pulled back for the truth to come forward. We must learn to love judgment and despise shame. Despise the foolishness of pride that hinders you from acknowledging defects in order to correct them and reach maturity. God is the potter and we are the clay. Our true selves can only be formed by the loving hands of God. Prior to surrendering to The Potter, our shape is from the pressures and influences of this present age. Our true selves are in the image of the eternal YAHWEH.

Don't Fight for the False

The process of being transformed into our true selves is what the apostle Paul speaks of in Romans 12:1–2 (KJV): "I beseech you therefore, brethren, by the mercies of God, that you present your bodies a living sacrifice, holy, acceptable to God, which is your reasonable service. And do not be conformed to this world, but be transformed by the renewing of your mind, that you may prove what is that good and acceptable and perfect will of God."

God wants us to bare His image, which is the mold of our true selves, to be a manifestation of His light in a world that has grown dark. We cannot allow the discomfort that comes with leaving the worldly things we are accustomed to, to become a source of resentment toward God.

It is natural to resist change. It is natural for a child to rebel against correction and reproof in foolish pride and ignorance. The process of rearing children is often sabotaged by the devil, through lying accusations directed at the parents. The lack of understanding, along with the pride and selfishness of the child is exploited by the devil. Sowing strife and discord through lying accusations is a common strategy of the devil. We see this in the book of Revelation, chapter 12, verses 9–10 (NKJV):

> So the great dragon was cast out, that serpent of old, called the Devil and Satan, who deceives the whole world; he was cast to the earth, and his angels were cast out with him. Then I heard a loud voice saying in heaven, Now salvation, and strength, and the kingdom of our God, and the power of His Christ have come, for the accuser of our brethren, who accused them before our God day and night, has been cast down.

Because of the blood of Yeshua, God no longer gives the devil audience; however, now Satan is roaming the earth, seeking an audience with us. Through the doors of ignorance, pride, and selfishness, Satan finds a captive audience. The devil can use the blindness of pride and selfishness to distort noblest of intentions to look like unfairness and neglect. Our Heavenly Father sometimes allows us to face challenges for an opportunity to discover our potential, however through lying accusations it can appear as cold abandonment. The lying deceit of pride and selfishness can convert loving correction into rejection. Correction and reproof will always come from loving parents and a loving God. A hardened heart is resistant to love.

The freedom sought through rebelling against God and godly parents actually leads to confinement. Herein lies the goal of the serpent, the devil, the deceiver, to keep us bound. The devil wants to keep us bound to our false self, bound to darkness, bound to the ways of this present age, to keep us from walking in the brightness of our Father's eternal glory. As eagle hatchlings peck their way out of shells, we must labor to get out of our false self. The hardness of the shell protected us when we were in a state of rebellion, fending for ourselves, but when we come to an understanding that we are in the care of the Lord, we can shed the hardness of selfishness and pride.

When you think about it, it really is the wings and plumage of the adult eagle that protects the eggs and keeps them safe, not so much the shell. The shell can't protect against the real predator that invades the nest. In the same way, it really has been God watching over us our whole lives, and not our own effort that has kept us from being destroyed by the devil. We must use the cross as a tool to help pick ourselves out of the shell of prideful and selfish living into the awareness of God's loving care. Yeshua taught that those that would follow him needed to take up their cross daily. Pride and selfishness limits us so much from experiencing the fullness of life, just like being in a shell.

Trusting God to Freedom

If we cannot trust the love of God to protect us in life, there is no way we are coming out of our shells. Until we learn to trust God, we will be dominated by the selfish orientation of self-preservation. If we cannot accept that we are dearly beloved of God, and precious in His sight, there is no way we are going to stop promoting our false selves in pride. There must be hope in God's love and trust that His intentions are always good toward us. We have to open ourselves to a love relationship with God that includes His chastisement and correction, which are necessary for our fulfillment. It is impossible to please God without the faith that works by the knowledge of His steadfast love. You will never surrender to the potter until you trust His loving hands, and you will never know freedom until He touches you.

Chapter 6

KNOW YOUR GOD

The Carnal Mind

Today I was part of a Bible study with men present who were unlearned in the Word of God. There were also men present who had been raised in the church, and others who were very read in the doctrines of Christianity. We were studying the Ten Commandments. One of the "younglings" in the gospel asked a question that stirred a lot of conversation in the group. The question was, "Why does God break his own commandments, in that he tells us not to murder, when he has slain men by the thousands?" To me, the answer was simple, with no need to go into deep apologetics, but there were many amongst the learned Christians who came to a consensus on an answer that wasn't very definitive. Their answer was, "God is mysterious and unfathomable."

Here is this neophyte, trying to understand the God he is being drawn to, and these supposed elders are telling him that God can't be understood or truly known. I know they meant well, but as iron sharpens iron, I sharply objected to that discourse, and proceeded to address the question. After the Bible study, as we all departed, I was given a book by one of the men who had come to a consensus with the others that God was unfathomable. It was a book written by A. W. Toser titled *The Knowledge of the Holy*. He encouraged me to read it, especially the chapter titled "God Incomprehensible." I read the chapter as soon as I arrived home, and it made me wonder if he had read it himself.

My take on the chapter was that God cannot be comprehended with the natural mind or mere intellect, but can only be understood via the new mind and heart after being born again. Somehow the brother who gave me the book thought it supported his view that God was simply incomprehensible. The whole concept of the Father being incomprehensible to his own children speaks volumes to me regarding the lack of genuine intimacy experienced by believers in their earthly family relationships, especially between children and their parents. It also gave me a fresh perspective on why our Saviour was almost stoned for saying what was recorded in John 10:30 (KJV): "I and my Father are one."

Obviously, many of the Jewish leaders who heard this proclamation from Yeshua also felt that God the Father was unfathomable, and beyond comprehension. This explains why they rent their clothes upon hearing this carpenter's son proclaim he embodied the very fullness of God. I get the feeling that there were men at the Bible study I mentioned earlier who would have reacted similarly.

Parting the Veil of the Flesh

Yeshua came and gave himself as a sacrifice to take away the partition between God and His lost children. The atoning blood of Christ makes it possible for the relationship between the Father and his children to be restored. Now the Father can sew His seed in our hearts and restore us to His image: "For this purpose the Son of God was manifested, that he might destroy the works of the devil" (1 John 3:8 KJV).

The work of the devil is to kill, steal, and destroy through spewing lies that divide and then conquer. The works of the devil are built upon his lies. Truth destroys the works of the wicked one. Those who are transformed into sons of God through faith in Yeshua walk in the Truth. The light of Truth annihilates the kingdom of darkness. Salvation is the act of being restored to the children of God so that His life courses through us. Satan in futility opposes this great threat. Now that the love of God through Yeshua has eliminated sin consciousness in His children and we draw near to God, Satan has found a new way to bring division in the relationship. Satan has spun divisive doctrines through religious organizations, telling men that it is impossible to know God, and that being godly and perfect is unattainable while having a fleshly body on earth.

These false doctrines have created a new veil between man and God. Those believing these false doctrines have put the gifts and promises purchased through the blood of Yeshua beyond reach. Acceptance of these doctrines distorts the image of God to someone no human can relate to, though we were made in His image. These doctrines created by the devil have produced a powerless religion that people put forward as Christianity. It is one of the main reasons why it is hard to tell the difference between those who confess to know Christ and those who do not. These false doctrines also imply that the nature of sin is more powerful than the life of God within born again believers. These doctrines keep believers from accepting the truth that Yeshua has freed us from the power of sin, and transformed our minds that we might apprehend the things of God.

In Romans 6:6–18 (NKJV), Paul explains:

Knowing this, that our old man was crucified with Him, that the body of sin might be done away with, that we should no longer be slaves of sin. For he who has died has been freed from sin.

Now if we died with Christ, we believe that we shall also live with Him, knowing that Christ, having been raised from the dead, dies no more. Death no longer

D.L. FULLER

has dominion over Him. For the death that He died, He died to sin once for all; but the life that He lives, He lives to God.

Likewise you also, reckon yourselves to be dead indeed to sin, but alive to God in Christ Jesus our Lord. Therefore do not let sin reign in your mortal body, that you should obey it in its lusts. And do not present your members as instruments of unrighteousness to sin, but present yourselves to God as being alive from the dead, and your members as instruments of righteousness to God. For sin shall not have dominion over you, for you are not under law but under grace.

What then? Shall we sin because we are not under law but under grace? Certainly not! Do you not know that to whom you present yourselves slaves to obey, you are that one's slaves whom you obey, whether of sin leading to death, or of obedience leading to righteousness? But God be thanked that though you were slaves of sin, yet you obeyed from the heart that form of doctrine to which you were delivered. And having been set free from sin, you became slaves of righteousness.

These verses tell us that if we surrender our will to God, and become open to the true choices that God has set before us, we have the opportunity *today* to be faithful servants of righteousness, and no longer slaves to sin. In spite of the clarity of these verses, if you ask the majority of believers if they can live sin-free, they will tell you that no man can. I realize that many believers are confused on this issue because they don't understand the difference in having a nature of sin versus acting out that skew toward sin in our lives. The topic of sin and salvation has become controversial due to the lies and deception of Satan, but there is no contradiction in truth, and the scriptures truly are in agreement on the point. What I am trying to establish is that the more you know the author of truth, the more you will "be able to comprehend with all saints what is the breadth, and length, and depth, and height" of the things of God (Ephesians 3:18 KJV).

Going on to Perfection

Sin is a spiritual issue, and it must be dealt with spiritually. The belief that being outside of flesh frees us from the influence of sin is simply not true. When Lucifer led a third of the angels in rebellion against God in heaven, none of them had fleshly bodies. There is a lot to be said on this subject, but to stay in context of our Godly heritage, it is important to know that through Christ we inherit God's holy nature. It is from this reality that God *commands* us to be holy, even as He is holy, and it is from this reality that God commands us to be perfect because He is perfect. The carnal mind cannot understand the things of the spirit. This was illustrated by Nicodemus in John 3:4 (NKJV), when he responded to Christ, stating the necessity of being born again. Nicodemus replied, "How can a man be born when he is old? Can he enter the second time into his mother's womb, and be born? Thinking to be born again meant entering again into the womb of your mother."

Similarly, when men think of perfection, they think of reaching a state where you have no impure thoughts, where you never say or do anything inappropriate, where you never miss the mark. This is not the "perfect" referred to in scripture. The scripture is referring to godliness and maturity. Look at Matthew 5:48 (AMP): "You, therefore, must be perfect [growing into complete maturity of godliness in mind and character, having reached the proper height of virtue and integrity], as your Heavenly Father is perfect."

Let's also look at Matthew 19:21 (KJV): "Jesus said unto him, If thou wilt be perfect, go and sell that thou hast, and give to the poor, and thou shalt have treasure in heaven: and come and follow me."

Are we to believe that the rich young ruler was flawless in every way except for the need to sell off all of his belongings for the poor? No, that's not it. He was not yet ready to be totally and singularly identified with Christ in his life. The Bible says that the rich young ruler went away grieved because he had great possessions. Matthew 6:20–22 (KJV) says, "But lay up for yourselves treasures in heaven, where neither moth nor rust doth corrupt, and where thieves do not break through nor steal: For where your treasure is, there will your heart be also. The light of the body is the eye: if therefore thine eye be single, thy whole body shall be full of light."

The rich young ruler was not ready to be filled with light, because his heart was divided. Every man has the potential to reach the point of total surrender where he realizes that all of life's true riches are obtained through following God. When a man has suffered enough disappointment and hurt from living according to his own ambitions and lust, he will hopefully come to the point of surrender. At this breaking point, if he decides to cry out to the Lord, then the Lord will save him and make him free by the power of His love. There are other choices at this breaking point that lead to destruction instead of life. These other choices are methods of anesthetizing the pain, such as altering the conscience through drugs, or trying to live immersed in carnal pleasures, or just giving up on life.

> Humble yourselves therefore under the mighty hand of God, that he may exalt you in due time: Casting all your care upon him; for he careth for you. Be sober, be vigilant; because your adversary the devil, as a roaring lion, walketh about, seeking whom he may devour: Whom resist stedfast in the faith, knowing that the same afflictions are accomplished in your brethren that are in the world. But the God of all grace, who

hath called us unto his eternal glory by Christ Jesus, after that ye have suffered a while, make you perfect, stablish, strengthen, settle you. To him be glory and dominion forever and ever. Amen. (1 Peter 5:7–11 KJV)

Once we become truly surrendered, our spirit, soul, and body find the right alignment, and focus on Jesus. Matthew 6:22 (KJV) says, "The light of the body is the eye: if therefore thine eye be single, thy whole body shall be full of light."

Now we are perfect once we are surrendered and get the correct alignment; however, the process of being filled with light is a redemptive promise that is realized congruently with our "knowing" of the Lord.

The Power of Intimacy

As we grow in our intimacy with God, or our knowing of God, the truth of God fortifies us against the power of Satan. The power of Satan is deception and lies. If we stand on the knowledge of God and resist Satan, then he will flee. In the book of Daniel, chapter 11, verse 32 states, "The people that do know their God shall be strong, and do exploits."

This *knowing* of God which leads to taking ground for the kingdom is not some vague understanding of an incomprehensible God, but rather a deep knowing that comes from a loving and intimate relationship. In Exodus 33:11 (KJV) we read, "And the Lord spake unto Moses face to face, as a man speaketh unto his friend. And he turned again into the camp: but his servant Joshua, the son of Nun, a young man, departed not out of the tabernacle."

We see Moses entering the Tabernacle and communing with YAHWEH as with a friend, however other men worshipped from their tents. There was one other in the tabernacle with Moses, young Joshua, the son of Nun. The scripture says when Moses left out of the tabernacle Joshua stayed behind, no doubt to also commune with God. The intimate knowledge of God was essential to Moses being able to stand against Pharaoh and to leading the rebellious children of Israel. Joshua, when he was older, led the children of Israel in glorious exploits, taking the land of Canaan in the name of the Lord. The expansion of God's kingdom on earth is facilitated through the intimacy of knowing Him. The assurance of God's amazing love enables men to stand and not faint in the face of adversity. Psalm 27:13–14 (KJV) says, "I had fainted, unless I had believed to see the goodness of the Lord in the land of the living. Wait on the Lord: be of good courage, and he shall strengthen thine heart: wait, I say, on the Lord."

Chapter 7

THE FIRM FOUNDATION

Establishing a Standard

Any structure that is going to be safe and reliable has to be built on a firm foundation. It is the same with the structure of our personality. If we are to be sound individuals, there are certain characteristics of our personality that need to remain consistent and immovable. It takes sound individuals to create stable families, and stable families make up the bedrock for productive, thriving civilizations. I would like to focus on the family environment since it is the foundation of any successful civilization. The dynamics of immediate family have the greatest impact on how we interact socially. Our family environment gives us the parameters by which we judge the outside world. As we interact socially with the world abroad, we measure with the ruler forged from experiences with our immediate family. A system of measure is only useful if its standards are consistent. The role of parents is to provide the consistent standards by which children can make up their rulers to build sound social structures like family, friendships, and business relationships. If all parents relied on the standards from God for this task, then the whole would be more functional and sounder. The cross of Yeshua is meant to calibrate all of us to God's standards. Psalm 127:1 (KJV) says, "Unless the Lord build the house they labor in vain, unless the Lord keeps the city the watchman waketh in vain."

Until we humbly embrace God's standards for living or the values God uses for measure, nothing we do will last or be sustainable. The values we set for our children have a profound impact on their future and the future of civilization. As a parent, this is extremely weighty. The weight of this responsibility, when you truly understand it, should make your knees buckle to the point you kneel and cry out to God. That is exactly what I did and why I constantly pray for guidance, wisdom, and knowledge in my parenting.

Godly Parents

Parents must realize that it is not their words that children internalize the most, it is their actions. Our children watch us constantly. That is how they often develop the same mannerisms, the same walk, and posture as their parents. Children are constantly watching and gathering material from their parents to build their rulers and standards for life. It takes a healthy marriage to create a healthy home environment for children. The role of mother and father are extremely important social roles. To have a healthy marriage, we must excel in our roles as husbands and wives. The person we arrive at as an adult will become the material used to build a healthy marriage, because you become part of a family structure. Even if we don't marry, we may take part in society as that mentor or dear friend who helps to shape others.

I see a cycle here. Who we become as an adult depends heavily on the upbringing we've had, which points back to what kind of people our parents became, which points back to their parents. This social cycle brings to the forefront the vital need for a solid and strong origination point. This is why the understanding of our Godly heritage is paramount to maintaining strong families unto productive, sound societies. When we understand our origin is YAHWEH, we can look to our Heavenly Father for the best, most consistent source for our standards of living and our truest character traits. Our earthly parents doing the best they can will still fall short in most cases of being flawless examples, but they can carry us adequately to a point where we are ready to walk with God, the Heavenly Father, ourselves. This is achieved by our parents living in the precepts and doctrines of God so that when children model the parents they are really modeling the holiness and righteousness of YAHWEH. The precepts and doctrines that make up YAHWEH's holiness and righteousness are immaculate and whole, lacking nothing, therefore they are unchanging. They are unchanging because they cannot be improved upon, and the ways of YAHWEH will never diminish. The character of YAHWEH is life. The character of YAHWEH is what makes up the vitality and vibrancy that sustains *eternal* life.

While setting forth the right examples, parents should also talk to their children about their heritage in God the Father, and how that is why we live in righteousness and holiness. As early as possible, children need to understand how they relate to God. The scriptures teach that the devil, as a roaring lion, goes about seeking whom he may devour. Well, we know that lions pray on the young, the weak, and the isolated. This equates to children being a primary target of the devil. Parents must teach their children truth, beginning when they are young, so they can be empowered early against the deceptions of the devil.

A child having an early understanding that they are an important *part* of a larger story may help them realize that they have a responsibility to God and everyone to be their best. An early understanding that everyone will answer to God for their actions might go a long way toward ascribing to God's values for life. Few parents take this approach to parenting. These days many parents feel that the child should find their own identity, so they fail to supply the proper signpost and signals that aid the child in arriving at the proper destination of a mature and sound individual. As a result, we have people in our society today building their standards for life on things that are unstable and temporal; like the man who has his manhood founded on his wealth or financial prowess; like the woman who gets her sense of worth from her physical beauty. The finances and wealth of this world are temporal and unstable, and physical beauty is fleeting.

Let us look at the first example of the man whose identity is tied to his money. What happens to this man when his business fails due to a change in the market? He becomes laden with insecurity as a man. A man afflicted with insecurity will often project those feeling on others by assuming that others think less of him. What will this man do to maintain his financial prowess? Almost anything! Many men have had their consciences seared in the pursuit of financial riches, or trying to maintain financial wealth. Whatever controls your identity has mastery over you.

Now let us look at the woman that has her identity tied to her physical beauty. She will constantly need her physical beauty affirmed in order to feel secure and accepted. This dependency could cause her to be overly critical of her body, leading to excessive accentuation of her physical attributes. The emphasis on her external appearance will likely create a lack of attention to her character as a person, the inner beauty. This shallowness could make her incapable of maintaining healthy relationships which she will probably attribute to being unattractive physically. This will then cause her to be even more self-conscious of her physical appearance. Many plastic surgeons make their living off this type of complex.

If you derive your sense of self-worth and identity from temporal things, you will never be a sound, stable person. For a man to make a good husband or father, he must be a stable person; this means his identity and values must have a firm foundation. For a woman to be a good wife or mother, her soul has to prosper; she has to realize that her true beauty and value lie in her good discretion and uniqueness as a virtuous woman. Early counsel from loving parents is crucial to establishing a foundation of good values that lead children to healthy, fulfilling, sustainable lives.

The parents of the man in our earlier example could have taught him 1 Timothy 6:10 (NKJV), which says, "For the love of money is a root of all kinds of evil, for which some have strayed from the faith in their greediness, and pierced themselves through with many sorrows."

The woman in our example could have been taught Proverbs 31:30 (KJV), "Charm is deceitful and beauty is passing, but a woman who fears the Lord, she shall be praised."

The man who builds his identity on Christ is like the man in Matthew 7:24–25 (KJV): "Therefore whosoever heareth these sayings of mine, and doeth them, I will liken him unto a wise man, which built his house upon a rock: And the rain descended, and the floods came, and the winds blew, and beat upon that house; and it fell not: for it was founded upon a rock."

So is the person that builds their identity on the Rock from which every man is hewn, God the father. God made all men in His image. This speaks to our character and nature as a people. This truth should be the standard that defines us. Unfortunately, there is a majority view among believers and non-believers that godliness is unattainable in this life. This perspective has to be cast down.

Chapter 8

CHOOSING SIDES

We all have a decision to make. Will we be identified with man after the flesh? Or God after the spirit? One choice will alienate us from man, and one choice will alienate us from God. This is why Yeshua said He came not to bring peace, but a sword.

In Matthew, chapter 10, verse 34, Yeshua gives counsel on this issue: "Do not think that I came to bring peace on earth. I did not come to bring peace but a sword. For I have come to set a man against his father, a daughter against her mother, and a daughter-in-law against her mother-in-law."

Yeshua is acknowledging that when we choose to be identified with Him after the spirit, the result will be division from those that live after the flesh, and in some cases, this may be a family member. It is tough sometimes coming to the realization that those whom we want to see in the best light are in darkness, and in some cases evil. Until we reach the decision that we will be identified with Christ above all else, we will experience a lot of internal conflict and dissonance. What has helped me to resolve this conflict is realizing only that which is of God is real anyway. We never truly lose anything when we side with Christ, because everything else is false and lifeless. We do not have the potential to grasp that which is real until we are willing to let go of that which is false. He that loses his life will find it. When we say we want the truth, we are in effect saying we don't want that which is false. Likewise, if we love the truth, then it follows that we despise that which is false.

When the truth about my identity started to be revealed to me, it brought about some realities that were very revolutionary. Here is an example. In the country of America, where I am striving to realize my citizenship, people of my ethnicity are called Black. Before, I saw myself as a Black man; however, now in light of truth, I see myself as a man, first and foremost. It is only in the perspective of being a full man first do I then acknowledge my ethnicity. So, instead of being a Black man, I am actually a man who is black. It is important that I first identify with my heritage as a man created in God's image, because this is my first and eternal reality, and it defines my true pedigree.

As the tree speaks to the potential of the seed, this spiritual truth defines the characteristics that should be evident in me as I mature, as well as the fruit I should produce. On the other hand, my physical heritage, which also includes my ethnicity, aligns me with particular challenges and predispositions that I must overcome in the pursuit of expressing my true self. There is no virtue in my physical body aside from the expressions of the spirit that shines through. This truth was illustrated in the life of King Nebuchadnezzar. He had to be abased because he failed to acknowledge that the greatness in his life was imparted to him by God. The anointing from the Spirit of God upon him was the source of his glory.

Daniel, chapter 4, verses 30–37 (KJV) read:

The king spoke, saying, "Is not this great Babylon, that I have built for a royal dwelling by my mighty power and for the honor of my majesty?"

While the word was still in the king's mouth, a voice fell from heaven: "King Nebuchadnezzar, to you it is spoken: the kingdom has departed from you!

And they shall drive you from men, and your dwelling shall be with the beasts of the field. They shall make you eat grass like oxen; and seven times shall pass over you, until you know that the Most High rules in the kingdom of men, and gives it to whomever He chooses."

That very hour the word was fulfilled concerning Nebuchadnezzar; he was driven from men and ate grass like oxen; his body was wet with the dew of heaven till his hair had grown like eagles' feathers and his nails like birds' claws.

And at the end of the time I, Nebuchadnezzar, lifted my eyes to heaven, and my understanding returned to me; and I blessed the Most High and praised and honored Him who lives forever: For His dominion is an everlasting dominion, And His kingdom is from generation to generation.

All the inhabitants of the earth are reputed as nothing; He does according to His will in the army of heaven and among the inhabitants of the earth. No one can restrain His hand or say to Him, "What have you done?"

At the same time my reason returned to me, and for the glory of my kingdom, my honor and splendor returned to me. My counselors and nobles resorted to me, I was restored to my kingdom, and excellent majesty was added to me.

Now I, Nebuchadnezzar, praise and extol and honor the King of heaven, all of whose works are truth, and

His ways justice. And those who walk in pride He is able to put down.

Earlier in this same chapter of Daniel, it is said that God took the *man* heart from King Nebuchadnezzar, and gave him the heart of a beast. The true heart of man reflects the majesty of God. My true self is expressed through the divine nature I inherited as a child of God, redeemed through the life of Yeshua the Christ. The bastard-ized heart reflects that of a devilish beast. Any person that glories in the physicality of their being is unwise, like King Nebuchadnezzar. It is vain to glory in one's race or physical stature. The true virtues of life are the attributes that come from the spirit of God. This is the message found in 2 Peter 1:2–11 (NKJV):

Grace and peace be multiplied to you in the knowl-edge of God and of Jesus our Lord, as His divine power has given to us all things that pertain to life and godliness, through the knowledge of Him who called us by glory and virtue, by which have been given to us exceedingly great and precious promises, that through these you may be partakers of the divine nature, having escaped the corruption that is in the world through lust.

But also for this very reason, giving all diligence, add to your faith virtue, to virtue knowledge, to knowl-edge self-control, to self-control perseverance, to per-severance godliness, to godliness brotherly kindness, and to brotherly kindness love. For if these things are yours and abound, you will be neither barren nor un-fruitful in the knowledge of our Lord Jesus Christ. For he who lacks these things is shortsighted, even to blindness, and has forgotten that he was cleansed from his old sins.

Therefore, brethren, be even more diligent to make your calling and election sure, for if you do these things you will never stumble; for so an entrance will be supplied to you abundantly into the everlasting kingdom of our Lord and Savior Yeshua the Christ.

When we answer the call to walk with Yeshua, He commands us to take up our cross. This cross is where we make the choice to crucify our carnal affinities that we might walk in newness of life, after His spirit and become partakers of His divine nature. The cross is where we make the choice to suffer in the flesh that we might prosper in the spirit. The cross is where we make the choice to die to the old man fashioned after the world, that we might give life to the new man created in the image of the heavenly. The cross is where we make the choice to turn from darkness to light. As we read in 2 Peter, the virtues of the spirit allow us to escape the blindness and corruption that lies in darkness. Without the illumination of the spirit, the entities in our existence are shrouded with darkness making our lives unintelligible. Lives outside of Yeshua are built upon theories, superstitions, estimates, and other uncertainties, mostly originated out of fear. We must choose to put our spiritual life as priority one.

I define myself first as a divine child of God after the life of the spirit, then I identify my role on earth by my sex (son, brother, husband, father), and I try to express my true self to the best of my spiritual capabilities. Anything else that I allow to define me beyond this point becomes a limitation. Physical dimensions, social status, environmental influences, fashion and trends, time and space, are all fleeting and changing properties of this current world that are too temporary to define an eternal being. As spiritual beings, it is perverse to put the temporal before eternal. Imagine a multi-trillionaire who gets hungry, and permanently exchanges all of his fortune for a picture of an apple. The things of this world are only reflections of the real things that lie in the spiritual realm. The carnal things of this world cannot satisfy the deep craving within us for real spiritual things like love, peace, and joy. That is why the Bible teaches us to lay up for ourselves treasures in heaven. We need to be about acquiring eternal things. This is also why some of the richest people are truly the poorest, and some of the poorest people truly are the richest. We have to choose if we will live according to the temporal, or if we will live according to the eternal. We have to choose if we will be identified with Christ and the eternal things of the spirit, or if we will hold on to our temporal carnal things of this present world. Will we be true or false? Will we be reconciled through Christ to our Heavenly Father, who alone is our true origin? Or will we continue to be children of the devil, who is the author and progenitor of all that is false?

We are spiritual beings created in the image of God who have lost our way due to intentional acts of deception by a wicked foe. Thanks be to God the Father who has sent Yeshua the Christ, the good shepherd, to recover all of the lost sheep, shining the light of eternal truth. Christ declared, "I am the way, the truth, and the life; no one comes to the Father except through me" (John 14:6 NKJV).

Because of Christ, we can now be reconciled to our true Father, and discover all that we are truly meant to be.

Chapter 9

THE FAMILY OF GOD

Show Us the Father

John 14:7–9 (NKJV) says, "'If you had known Me, you would have known My Father also; and from now on you know Him and have seen Him.' Philip said to Him, 'Lord, show us the Father, and it is sufficient for us.' Yeshua said to him, 'Have I been with you so long, and yet you have not known Me, Philip? He who has seen Me has seen the Father; so how can you say, "Show us the Father"?'"

There is a mystery surrounding family, just as there is a mystery surrounding marriage. In the book of Ephesians, chapter 5, we learn about the mystery of marriage. In the book of Ephesians, chapter 3, we learn about the mystery of family.

> For this reason I bow my knees to the Father of our Lord Jesus Christ, from whom the whole family in heaven and earth is named, that He would grant you, according to the riches of His glory, to be strengthened with might through His Spirit in the inner man, that Christ may dwell in your hearts through faith; that you, being rooted and grounded in love, may be able to comprehend with all the saints what is the width and length and depth and height, to know the love of Christ which passes knowledge; that you may

be filled with all the fullness of God. (Ephesians 3:14–19 NKJV)

The love expressed through the life of Christ is nothing less than the manifest love of God the Father reaching out to His children. In the mystery of marriage, a principle we learn is that husbands should love their wives as Christ loved the church. A principle we learn in the mystery of family is that earthly fathers should love their children as the Heavenly Father loves His. A lot of what we see today in the deterioration of family and the lack of family values are the results of men not understanding the mystery of family. Men have to be able to relate their role as fathers with the acts of God throughout the Bible. We have to be able to relate the expressed love through Christ as the love of the Father for his children. This is clearly expressed in 2 Corinthians 5:18–20 (NKJV): "Now all things are of God, who has reconciled us to Himself through Jesus the Christ, and has given us the ministry of reconciliation, that is, that God was in Christ reconciling the world to Himself, not imputing their trespasses to them, and has committed to us the word of reconciliation."

The outstretched arms of Yeshua are the open arms of God the Father, calling all his children back into unity with Him. Once we become grounded in the revelation that Yeshua is the express image of the Father, then we can begin to really understand the continuity of the gospel from Genesis to revelation.

Throughout the ages, God has been restoring his family, from the initial rift in the Garden with Adam to the day of Pentecost when the Holy Spirit began the ministry of revealing the love of God the Father in the hearts of men. God has been manifest throughout time as God the Father, God the Son, and God the Holy Spirit, with *one* love. However, the persona of God the Father seems to be locked in the Old Testament with the great flood, the destruction of Sodom and Gomorrah, the plagues of Egypt, and the wrathful annihilation of thousands. This disconnect is also evident in the popular portrayal of Yeshua as the lamb of God, and that he is, but he is also the

Lion of Judah. Everything that the Father is, Yeshua is as well, and everything that Yeshua is, the Father is as well. Yeshua declared that he and the Father were one.

Knowing the Father

After we are reconciled back to the Father through Yeshua, it is like a branch being grafted back into the vine from which it came. The sap of the vine begins to nourish the reconciled branch, and inevitably it starts to bear fruit again. This is what Paul is saying to the Ephesians in chapter 3, verses 17–19 (NKJV): "Being rooted and grounded in love, may be able to comprehend with all the saints what is the width and length and depth and height, to know the love of Christ which passes knowledge; that you may be filled with all the fullness of God."

In other words, Paul is talking about being reconciled back into the family of God, and then having the Holy Spirit fill you, and reveal the love of the Father in your heart. This love, like a healing balm, restores your heart from all its injuries; the injuries of hate, rejection, and dejection, received from a life outside the refuge God's love. The provisions of God's love are always available, but man is not always in a place to receive what God is offering. Man's perception is often distorted due to his broken heart. Our perception of the world around us is based on the condition of our heart on the inside. The heart is what gives dimension and meaning to what we perceive. A wounded heart causes distortion of truth. As the heart is restored, we regain the ability to perceive truth, which allows for the renewing of the mind. Once we are able to comprehend the redemptive work God is accomplishing through salvation, then we begin to expect with everyday a changing in us from glory to glory, a transformation to the image and likeness of God, our father. The revelation of the love of the Father allows you to embrace 1 Peter 2:8–10 (NKJV):

"But you are a chosen generation, a royal priesthood, a holy nation, His own special people, that you may proclaim the praises of Him who called you out of darkness into His marvelous light; who once were not a people but are now the people of God, who had not obtained mercy but now have obtained mercy."

By the power of God, you can amount to more than the sum of your experiences thus far in life, no matter your age. With the Lord, a day is as a thousand years, and a thousand years is as one day. Spend as much time as you can in meditation on God's word and praying, developing intimacy with God the Father. From this intimacy you will become rooted and grounded in God's love. This love will produce a faith that is able to accept the truths of God, and you will be as one of the blind men receiving his sight in the book of Matthew, chapter 9. The Lord will say to you, "According to your faith be it unto you." (Matthew 9:29 KJV). Your faith in God's love will bring all of His promises within reach. This includes the promise of becoming a true son of God whereby you walk in God's likeness by inheritance. Allow the amazing grace of God, in the face of Yeshua the Christ, to persuade your heart unto belief and full acceptance of your true heritage in all of its glory.

ABOUT THE AUTHOR
D.L. FULLER

D euntray L. Fuller's life began at age 19 when he answered, "now" to the very direct and personal question posed to him by the spirit of God. The question was, "When are you going to sur-render ALL to me."

Fuller had gone to an alter call and acknowledged the need for salvation almost a year earlier, however he wasn't willing to take up his own cross until he was broken by YAHWEH's relentless show-ering of grace, mercy, and love. The revelation of YAHWEH in the face of Yeshua, persuaded Fuller that God rightfully deserved every milligram of his devotion. Fuller has been active in ministry ever since, from traditional neighborhood churches, to outreach minis-tries focusing on the homeless, drug addicted, and disenfranchised.

The practice of journaling the revelations of the spirit has been a constant in Fuller's life throughout his salvation experi-ence. Six years ago, Fuller was inspired to share the content of his journals in the form of this book, as well as a blog. The blog is "theinscribedheart.com." There you can find over a hundred diverse articles ranging from apologetics and poetry, to spiritual reflections on current events.

D.L. Fuller has been married for over thirty years to his bride Pamela. Together they have four children, Shaina, Jah'son, Amari, and Andrew.